# MACMILLAN
# NEXT
# MOVE
# 3

## Pupil's Book

**Amanda Cant   Mary Charrington**

# Contents

| | **Vocabulary** | **Grammar** | **Features** |
|---|---|---|---|
|  **Unit 1** pages 5–14 | exploring, climbing, drawing, watching TV, swimming, singing, playing football cute, athletic, friendly, strong, funny, smart | Let's go to the … Let's go by … (I sit) in front of / next to / behind (Oona.) | **Country:** Mexico **World Music Song:** The High Five Song **Phonics:** ar, all or |
| 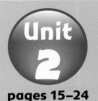 **Unit 2** pages 15–24 | eggs, cupcakes, sausages, crisps, cherries, strawberries, avocados, grapes soup, rice, bread, cereal, milk, fizzy drink, chocolate, pasta | There are some …–s. There aren't any …–s. There's some … There isn't any … Is there any …? Yes, there is. / No, there isn't. | **Country:** South Africa **World Music Song:** No Sausages! **Phonics:** br, sn, cl |
|  **Unit 3** pages 25–34 | Turkey, Turkish, South Korea, South Korean, Malaysia, Malaysian, the USA, American, Spain, Spanish, Japan, Japanese, the UK, British, India, Indian eat, drink, cook, sleep, wash, write | Where are you from? I'm / We're from … He's / She's / It's from … He's / She's / It's (nationality). Eat with me / us. Can I write to you? Let's sing with him / her. Climb it / them. | **Country:** Malaysia **World Music Song:** Travel Song **Phonics:** fr, bl, lk |
|  **Unit 4** pages 35–44 | ride, dive, climb, surf, fish, skate, ski, skateboard ping pong, tennis, baseball, football, ice hockey, basketball | I'm / We're …–ing. I'm not …–ing. We aren't …–ing. Are you / they …–ing? Yes, I am. / No, I'm not. Yes, they are. / No, they aren't. | **Country:** Italy **World Music Song:** Cool Sports **Phonics:** sk, sw, str |
|  **Unit 5** pages 45–54 | hot, rainy, sunny, cold, foggy, cloudy, windy, snowy dress, shorts, T-shirt, jeans, socks, boots | What's he / she / it doing? He's / She's …–ing. He's / She's / It's …–ing. He isn't / She isn't / It isn't …–ing. Is he/she …–ing? Yes, he / she is. /No, he/she isn't. | **Country:** Jamaica **World Music Song:** The Island Song **Phonics:** oo, ir, ow |

| Vocabulary | Grammar | Features |
|---|---|---|

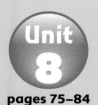

# Characters and Icons

## Activity Icons

**Audio**
Audio tracks to practise listening skills

**World Music**
Songs with a World Music flavour

**Template**
Photocopiable Presentation Files to use with Lesson 8

**Test Prep**
Exam style activities

Hi! My name's Zac. Do you like exploring? I do! Are you ready to go places? Are you ready to learn English?

I'm Oona! I'm Zac's friend. I love exploring! Come on, let's go!

## Competency Development Icons

**Me**
Activities that develop social and creative skills and foster intrapersonal intelligence

**Think**
Activities that develop critical thinking skills in identifying, processing and manipulating information

**Learn**
Activities that build learner autonomy and promote the use of learning strategies

**Collaborate / Communicate**
Activities that develop collaborative skills through teamwork and effective communication

**Act**
Activities that create societal understanding by promoting tolerance and ethical behaviour

4

Mexico

Welcome to Mexico!

We like exploring.
Let's explore the ocean.

Zoom In

He's in the Pacific Ocean in Mexico!

What are the five oceans in the world?
Which ocean creatures do you know?
Do you live near the ocean?

**Look at the picture.**
Can you think of three
things the diver can see?

Unit 1

# Lesson 1

**1** Listen and read.

**1**

Hi, Oona. How are you?

I'm fine, thanks.

**2**

I like exploring.

Me, too!

**2** Tick (✔) the activities you like, then say.

- ☐ exploring
- ☐ swimming
- ☐ climbing
- ☐ singing
- ☐ drawing
- ☐ playing football
- ☐ watching TV

# Unit 1 Lesson 2

 Track 3

**1** Listen, read and say.

**1**

Let's go to the desert and ride a donkey.

**2**

Train Station | Bus Station

OK. Let's go by train.

Let's go by bus.

**3**

Let's go by plane!

Good idea!

**Discover Grammar**

Let's go **by** + place / transport
Let's go **to** + place / transport

 Track 4

**2** Listen and say *Let's go by …* or *Let's go to …*

**3** Complete and say.

**1**

REPTILES

Let's go _____.

**3**

Let's go _____.

**2**

Now showing

Let's go _____.

**4**

TAXI

TAXI

Let's go _____.

Workbook page 5     Grammar Guide page 106

Unit 1 Lesson 3

Track 5

**1** Listen and chant.

**ar   all   or**

I'm in the park.
I have a guitar!

I'm in the mall.
I have a new ball.

Where am I this morning?
I'm exploring!

Track 6

**2** Listen and complete. Then cross (✘) out the word with a different sound.

| 1 guitar | 2 m__ __ ning | 3 m __ __ __ |
|---|---|---|
| m __ __ __ | expl __ __ ing | p __ __ k |
| b __ __ __ | p __ __ k | guit __ __ |
| _____ | _____ | _____ |

 **3** Add one more word to each column.

Workbook page 6

# Lesson 4

 **1** Listen and read.

**1**

Please don't run in the mall.

**2**
Hey! Don't drop litter in the park!

**3**

Sit down, Marty.

**4**

Ouch!

**2** Read the story again. Tick (✔) the **value**.

**Respect:** Listen to others. ☐ Listen to yourself. ☐

 **3** Think and answer.

Are you good at listening to others? Circle.   Yes / No

Who do you listen to? _____  _____  _____

# Unit 1 — Lesson 5

**Track 8**

**1** Listen, point and say.

1 cute
2 athletic
3 friendly
4 smart
5 funny
6 strong

**2** Put the words into the correct column.

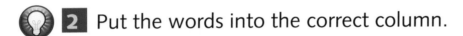

| Physical appearance | Characteristics |
| --- | --- |
| | |
| | |
| | |

**Track 9**

**3** Listen and sing. Make a new verse. **The High Five Song**

Let's High Five!
I'm smart,
You're smart,
We're all smart today.

Friends are smart!
Friends are cool,
Let's be friends,
At our school.

Let's High Five!
I'm strong,
You're strong,
We're all strong today.

_____

_____

_____

_____

10

**Unit 1**

# Lesson 6

**Grammar**

The city is **next to** the ocean.
The jungle is **behind** the city.
The pyramid is **in front of** the mountain.

Track 10

**1** Listen, read and say.

Zac is on a plane and he can see lots of things. There's a city next to the ocean. There's a jungle behind the city and there's a pyramid in front of a mountain.

But he can't see Oona under the plane.

**Discover Grammar**

Read. Then circle.

Alan sits **behind** me and **next to** Ben.
The sentence is talking about time / place.

**2**  Look and write.

**1** Where is the city? _____ .

**2** Where is the jungle? _____ .

**3** Where is the pyramid? _____ .

**3**  Play the Guessing Game.

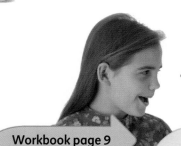

This person is friendly. She sits behind Al.

It's Sofia.

# Let's visit ... Mexico!

**1** Read about green iguanas from Mexico.

> ### IT'S A FACT!
>
> Iguanas can be two metres long! How tall are you? Green iguanas are lizards and they live in Mexico. They aren't very friendly, but they're smart and they're strong, too. They can climb trees and they can swim. They have short legs, a big head and a very long tongue. They like eating leaves, flowers and fruit for breakfast, lunch and dinner!

**2** Find out and write about iguanas.

| Characteristics | |
|---|---|
| Abilities | |
| Habits | |
| Physical appearance | |

## Think Twice

1   Do you like iguanas? Do you think they're interesting?
2   Why do you think iguanas are green and brown?

**Presentation: Tell your class about an animal from your country.**

Template 1

**1 Prepare.**

**Find information about your animal.**

- Choose an animal from your country.
- Draw a picture and label it.
- Find information about it.

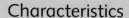

| Characteristics | |
| --- | --- |
| Abilities | |
| Habits | |
| Physical appearance | |

**2 Practise.**

**Describe your animal.**

| Let me tell you about ... | They live in ... | They have ... |
| --- | --- | --- |
| They are ... | They can ... | They like eating ... |

Track 11

**3 Present.**

Let me tell you about brown bears. They live in the mountains. They have big bodies and strong legs. They like eating fish and small mammals. They can swim, but they can't climb trees.

# Unit 1

**TEST PREP**

**1** Unscramble and write.

**1** go by Let's boat. _____

**2** by go car Let's. _____

**3** train Let's go by. _____

**4** go the to jungle Let's. _____    /4

**2** Read and write *Yes* or *No*.

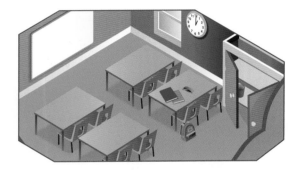

**1** There's a cupboard in front of the board. _____

**2** There's a clock next to the window. _____

**3** There's a board behind the desks. _____

**4** There are two books next to the pencil case. _____

**5** There's a school bag in front of a chair. _____

**6** There's a rubbish bin behind the door. _____    /6

Total score    /10

### My Progress

I can say sentences with *Let's* …    ✓ ? ✗

I can describe myself with two words.    ✓ ? ✗

I can read and say words with *ar*, *all* and *or*.    ✓ ? ✗

South Africa

We're in South Africa.
Look at the beautiful giraffe.

**Zoom In**

This giraffe lives in South Africa.

What other countries do giraffes live in?
What is the giraffe eating?
What else does it eat?
Do you have giraffes in your country?

**Look at the picture.**
Why do you think giraffes have long necks?

Unit 2

# Unit 2 Lesson 1

**Track 12**

**1** Listen, point and say.

1 strawberries
2 cherries
3 avocados
4 grapes
5 crisps
6 eggs
7 sausages
8 cupcakes

**2** Write sentences using *I like* and *I don't like*.

☺

1 _I like ..._____.
2 _____.
3 _____.
4 _____.

☹

5 _I don't like ..._____.
6 _____
7 _____
8 _____

**3** Talk to a friend.

Cupcakes!

Do you like cupcakes?

C-u-p-c-a-k-e-s.

Yes, I do.

16

# Unit 2 — Lesson 2

**Grammar**
There are **some** sausages.
There aren't **any** cherries.

**Track 13**

**1** Listen, read and say.

Zac and Oona are on safari and it's time for lunch.

Look at this picnic! There are some sausages and some sandwiches.

There aren't any strawberries and there aren't any cherries.

But there are some lions!

**Discover Grammar**

Circle.

There's + **some** / **any** ...

There isn't + **some** / **any** ...

**2** Look at Activity 1. Complete the sentences with *are*, *some* or *aren't any*.

1 There _____ apples.

2 There _____ cupcakes.

3 There _____ eggs.

4 There _____ pears.

**3** Play the Memory Game.

There are some sausages.

Yes!

# Unit 2 Lesson 3

**1** Listen and chant.

## br    sn    cl

Sara gets up at seven o'clock.
It's a very cloudy day.
For breakfast she has bread.
She's hungry today!

Sara's at the library.
Brian the snake is there.
They read a book and have a snack,
Some cupcakes and a pear.

**2** Circle, sort and write.

b r e a k f a s t s n a c k s n a k e c l o c k c l o u d y l i b r a r y

**br**                    **sn**                    **cl**

_____        _____        _____

_____        _____        _____

**3** Write a word with *br*, *sn* or *cl*.

___brown___        _____        _____

# Unit 2 Lesson 4

**Track 15**

**1** Listen and read.

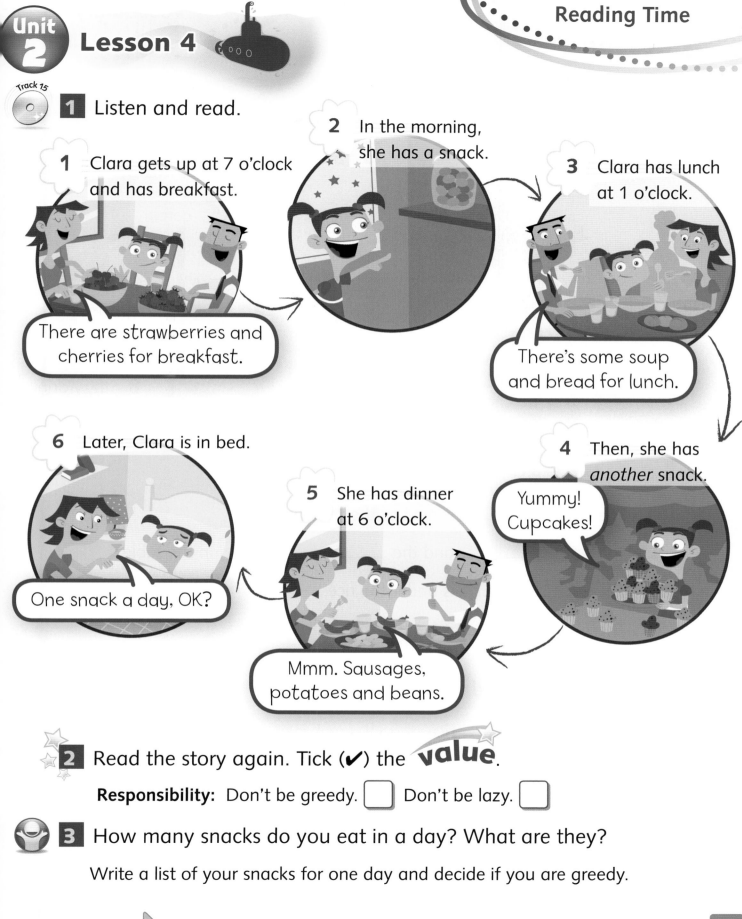

**1** Clara gets up at 7 o'clock and has breakfast.

There are strawberries and cherries for breakfast.

**2** In the morning, she has a snack.

**3** Clara has lunch at 1 o'clock.

There's some soup and bread for lunch.

**6** Later, Clara is in bed.

One snack a day, OK?

**5** She has dinner at 6 o'clock.

Mmm. Sausages, potatoes and beans.

**4** Then, she has *another* snack.

Yummy! Cupcakes!

**2** Read the story again. Tick (✔) the **value**.

**Responsibility:** Don't be greedy. ☐ Don't be lazy. ☐

**3** How many snacks do you eat in a day? What are they?

Write a list of your snacks for one day and decide if you are greedy.

# Unit 2 Lesson 5

**Track 16**

**1** Listen, point and say.

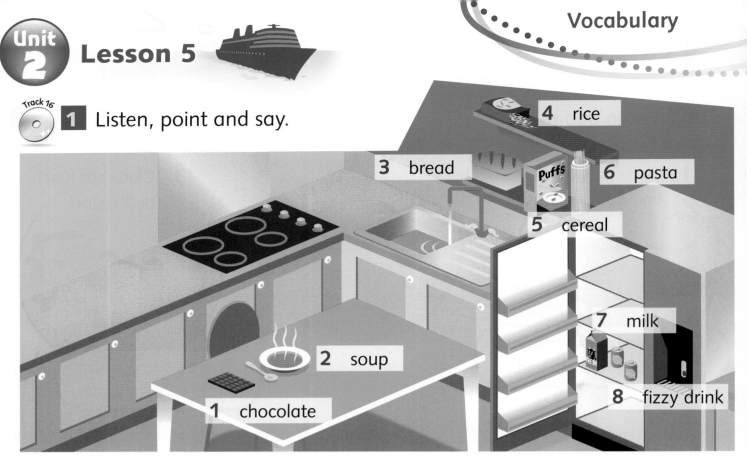

4 rice
3 bread
6 pasta
5 cereal
7 milk
2 soup
8 fizzy drink
1 chocolate

**2** Complete the sentences.

1 The _____ is next to the fizzy drink.

2 The _____ and the _____ are on the table.

3 The _____ is under the rice.

4 The _____ is next to the pasta.

**3** Write the foods and say.

> soup  pancakes  rice  apples  bread  cereal  sandwiches
> potatoes  milk  fish  eggs  pasta  juice  tomatoes  fizzy drink

In my house, we have _____ for breakfast.

In my house, we have _____ for lunch.

In my house, we have _____ for dinner.

> In my house, we have cereal for breakfast.

**Grammar** There's some / There isn't any …
Is there any rice?
Yes, **there is**. / No, **there isn't**.

 Track 17

**1** Listen, read and say.

It's 8 o'clock and it's dinner time.

Mmm, there's pasta and there's fruit.

There isn't any fizzy drink.

But there *is* some milk!

**Discover Grammar**

Circle.

There's + **some** / **any** …
There isn't + **some** / **any** …
Is there + **some** / **any** … ?

**2** Ask and answer.

Is there any …?    Yes, there is. / No, there isn't.

**1** chocolate   **2** milk   **3** cereal   **4** bread   **5** soup   **6** rice

 Track 18

**3** Listen and sing. **No Sausages!**

There aren't any sausages,
There isn't any rice,
There aren't any potato crisps,
And I think they're nice!

*Chorus*
But …
There are some eggs, 1, 2, 3,
And there is some bread,
Just for me!

**Unit 2** Lesson 7

Let's visit ...

# South Africa!

**1** Read about food in South Africa.

**IT'S A FACT!**

One ostrich egg weighs the same as about 24 chicken eggs!

## Big Breakfast

Many children all over the world have cereal, toast and eggs for breakfast. But in South Africa, if you go to an ostrich farm, there are omelettes on the breakfast menu – very big omelettes made from ostrich eggs! Ostrich eggs taste the same as chicken eggs, but they have very hard shells. You can jump on an ostrich egg and it won't break! Children in South Africa eat really delicious and healthy food for lunch and dinner. There are traditional meat, chicken and fish dishes and lots of healthy snacks like cherries, strawberries and grapes.

**2** Find and write.

1 What three things do many children have for breakfast?
2 Why are some omelettes special in South Africa?
3 What snacks do South African children eat?

## Think Twice

1 Compare your breakfast with a South African breakfast. Are they similar? What's different?
2 Why do you think it is important for ostrich eggs to have such hard shells?

# Lesson 8

 **Presentation: A meal in your country.**

**1 Prepare.**

**Find information about the meal.**

- Choose a typical meal from your country.
- Draw a picture and label it.
- Find information about it.

| Ingredients | Taste | Special characteristics |
|---|---|---|
|  |  |  |

**2 Practise.**

**Describe your typical meal.**

Let me tell you about ...        It has ... in it.

It's hot / cold.        It is salty / sweet.

**3 Present.**

Let me tell you about my favourite breakfast – it's delicious. It's cereal and there's some fruit in it – like strawberries or maybe some cherries. I have some bread with butter. To drink, I have some apple juice – it's nice and sweet. My breakfast is yummy!

Breakfast

## Progress check

**1** Read the story and write the words.

**TEST PREP**

Billy is a very greedy boy. Today he has a big breakfast. He has some ¹  ___cereal___

with milk, then some fruit – some ²  _____.

At school, he has a snack. He has some ³  _____ and some orange juice.

For lunch, he has potatoes, beans and some ⁴  _____. After school, he

has four ⁵  _____ and a ⁶ _____. Then Billy feels sick!

/5

**2** Look at the picture and write sentences.

There's some … There isn't any … There are some … There aren't any …

1  <u>There's some</u> _____ bread.

2  _____ milk.

3  _____ ice cream.

4  _____ sandwiches.

5  _____ crisps.

6  _____ soup.

/5

Total score  /10

**My Progress**

I can say sentences with There isn't / aren't any …

I can name five foods.

I can read and say words with *br*, *sn* and *cl*.

# Unit 3 · Lesson 1

**Track 20**

**1** Listen, point and say.

| | |
|---|---|
| 1 Turkey | Turkish |
| 2 South Korea | South Korean |
| 3 Malaysia | Malaysian |
| 4 the USA | American |
| 5 Spain | Spanish |
| 6 Japan | Japanese |
| 7 the UK | British |
| 8 India | Indian |

**2** Complete the sentences.

1 The _____ and the _____ flags are red and white.

2 The _____ and the _____ flags are red, blue and white.

3 The _____ flag is red, blue, white and yellow.

4 The _____ flag is orange, green, white and blue.

**3** Talk about a flag with your friend.

This flag is from Malaysia.

It's red, blue, white and yellow.

# Lesson 2

**1** Listen, read and say.

**Grammar**

**Where are you from?**
**I'm from** Mexico. **I'm** Mexican.
**Where's he / she from?**
**He's / She's from** Spain.
**He's / She's** Spanish.

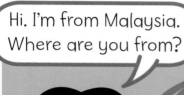
Hi. I'm from Malaysia. Where are you from?

I'm from the UK. This is Oona. She's Malaysian, too.

We're from Malaysia!

**Discover Grammar**

Circle.

We're from + **Turkey / Turkish.**
We're + **Turkey / Turkish.**

**2** Circle, then ask and answer.

| | | | |
|---|---|---|---|
| **1** | Where are pandas from? | They're from | India. / China. |
| **2** | Where are burgers from? | They're from | the USA. / Turkey. |
| **3** | Where's origami from? | It's from | Japan. / Russia. |

**3** Complete.

**1**  <u>Where are</u> they <u>from</u>?

They're from _____. They're _____.

**2**  _____ she _____?

She's from _____. She's _____.

# Unit 3 Lesson 3

**Track 22**

**1** Listen and chant.

**fr     bl     lk**

Freddie the frog is a friendly frog from France.

Blackie is a black and blue bird.

Wilkie makes milkshakes like silk! Mmm!

**Track 23**

**2** Listen and complete. Then cross (✗) out the word with a different sound.

1   mi <u>l</u> <u>k</u> shake

___ ___ og

___ ___ iendly

_____

2   ___ ___ ack

___ ___ iendly

___ ___ ue

_____

3   mi ___ ___ shake

si ___ ___

___ ___ ack

_____

**3** Look at the chant. Find one more word for each column.

**1** Listen and read.

**1**

INTERNATIONAL STUDENTS WELCOME

Welcome to the party. Where are you from?

We're from China.

We're from Russia.

We're from Kenya.

**2**

I like your blue silk dress.

Thank you. I like your black bag.

Thanks! Where are you from?

I'm from India.

**3**

Oh ... where are you from?

We're from Mars.

Well, you're welcome, too. We're all friends here!

**2** Read again. Tick (✔) the **value**.

**Diversity:** Talk to friendly people. ☐  Welcome different people. ☐

**3** How do you welcome new people? Read and tick (✔).

Say *hello* and your name. ☐        Help them with new things. ☐

Look at them. ☐        Invite them to a party. ☐

# Unit 3 Lesson 5

**Track 25**

**1** Listen, point and say.

**1** eat

**2** cook

**3** wash

**4** drink

**5** sleep

**6** write

**Track 26**

**2** Listen and answer *Yes, I do* or *No, I don't*.

**3** Complete the survey. Then talk to the class.

| | Me | Friend 1: | Friend 2: |
|---|---|---|---|
| Do you eat lunch at school? | | | |
| Do you drink milk for breakfast? | | | |
| Do you cook your dinner every day? | | | |
| Do you sleep with the door open? | | | |
| Do you wash your hair every day? | | | |
| Do you write in English every day? | | | |

We eat our lunch at school. I drink milk for breakfast. Maria doesn't drink milk for breakfast.

# Unit 3 — Lesson 6

Track 27

**1** Listen, read and say.

**1**

Look at that mountain! Let's climb it.

**2**

Look at those girls. Let's sing with them.

Can we sing with you?

Yes. Sing with us!

**3**

Look at that boy. Let's play football with him.

Come on! Play football with me!

**4**

Look at that girl. Let's help her.

**5**

What a busy day!

**Discover Grammar**

Tick (✔).

_____ They like    **I / you / he / she / it / we / they.**

_____ They like    **me / you / him / her / it / us / them.**

Track 28

**2** Listen and complete. Then sing. **Travel Song**

I'm with _____ ,
And you're with _____ ,
We're together in a boat on the blue, blue sea.

She's with _____ ,
And he's with _____ ,
They're together in a helicopter.

We're with _____ ,
And you're with _____ ,
We're together on a yellow school bus.

# Unit 3 — Lesson 7

## Let's visit ... Malaysia!

**1** Read about a special festival in Malaysia.

📁 **Mail** 🔍

Dear Pen Pal,

My name's Pao-Pei. I'm nine years old and I live in Pasir-Gudang, in Malaysia. I want to tell you about a special festival in my hometown. Every year we have an international kite festival in February. Kites are very popular in Malaysia. Are they popular in your country? People from all over the world, including Germany, the USA and Taiwan, visit us for our colourful festival. The kites are fantastic; they're beautiful.

Please tell me about a festival in your country.

Write to me soon,

Pao-Pei

*Fly a kite with me!*

**IT'S A FACT!**

Kite flying is a very old tradition in Asia – more than 2,300 years old!

**2** Read and answer.

1 What is Pao-Pei's nationality?
2 Find words she uses to describe the festival and the kites.
3 Can you describe the kite in the picture?

## Think Twice

1 Compare the kite festival to a festival in your country. How is it the same or different?
2 How do festivals help you to understand other people?

## Presentation: A festival in your country.

Template 3

**1** **Prepare.**

**Find information about the festival.**
**Use the questions to help you.**

- Choose a festival from your country.
- Draw a picture and label it.
- Find information about it.

What is the festival called?
What happens at the festival?

What do we say?
Why do you like it?

**2** **Practise.**

Let me tell you about ...        We give ...

We say ...        I like the festival because ...

Track 29

**3** **Present.**

Mummy

Let me tell you about Mother's Day.
It's a special festival for mothers.
Lots of countries celebrate Mother's
Day. We give presents (to our mums)
and we say 'Happy Mother's Day'.
This card and these flowers are for
my mum. I like Mother's Day because
I love my mum.

Happy
Mother's
Day

**Unit 3**

**TEST PREP**

**1** Unscramble, then write.

1 aimasayl  ___Malaysia___  ___He's Malaysian___ .

2 ketyur  _____  _____ .

3 het sua  _____  _____ .

4 comiex  _____  _____ .

5 pajan  _____  _____ .

6 asnip  _____  _____ .

/5

**2** Complete using words from the box.

> me    us    him    her    it    them    you

1 I can see Zac. He's waving to _____me_____.

2 Where's your sister? I can't see _____.

3 There are some cherries. Can you pass _____ to me, please?

4 From up here we can see our friends, but they can't see _____.

5 I love chocolate. Do you like _____, too?

6 Paul is my brother. Do you know _____?

/5

Total score  /10

## My Progress

I can name three countries and nationalities.  ✓ ? ✗

I can say a sentence using him or her.  ✓ ? ✗

I can say words with *be*, *fr* and *lk*.  ✓ ? ✗

# Italy

We're in Venice, Italy! Let's explore!

Here we go!

## Zoom In

This is a type of boat in Venice. It's called a gondola.

What do you know about Italy?

Can you name some famous food from Italy?

What types of transport do people use in your country?

**Look at the picture.**
How are the people in the picture travelling? Why?

# Unit 4

# Unit 4   Lesson 1

Track 30

**1** Listen, point and say.

ride   dive   climb   ski   surf   fish   skate   skateboard

**2** Circle the correct word.

**1** You can        surf / ride horses        in the ocean.

**2** You can        fish / dive              in a pool.

**3** You can        ski / skateboard         in the mountains.

**4** You can        skate / climb            in the mountains.

**3** Check your answers with a friend.

Can you skateboard in the ocean?

No, you can't.

36

Workbook page 28

**1** Listen, read and say.

**Grammar** I'm fish**ing**. **I'm not** swimm**ing**.
**We're** sail**ing**. **We aren't** walk**ing**.

Zac and Oona are in Italy.

Look! We're sailing in a boat. We aren't swimming.

And I'm fishing, too!

**Discover Grammar**

**Circle.**

To say what is happening now, we use:

I'm + **climb / climbing.**

We aren't + **ride / riding.**

**2** Write sentences.

I _____ riding a horse.

I _____ surfing.

We _____ fishing.

We _____ climbing.

We're walking

**3** Act it out. Then say.

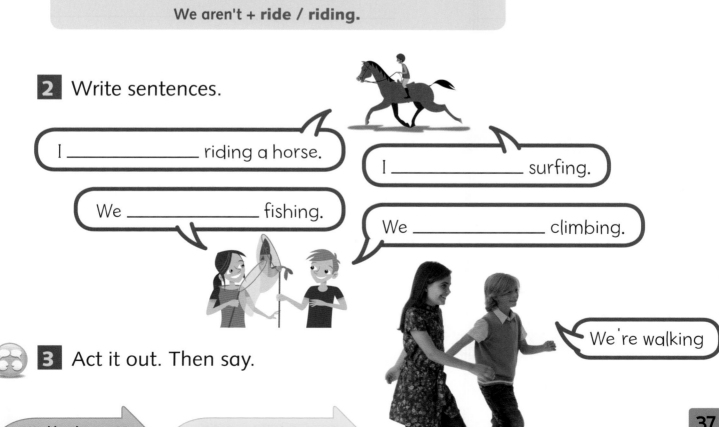

Workbook page 29    Grammar Guide page 107

# Unit 4 — Lesson 3

 **1** Listen and chant.

Track 32

## sk    sw    str

Skyler is strong. What can she do?
She can swim and skate very well,
And she can ski, too!

Skyler is hungry. What can she eat?
Strawberries and cream,
And something very sweet!

 **2** Circle, then sort and write.

| str | sw | sk |
|---|---|---|
| _____ | _____ | _____ |
| _____ | _____ | _____ |

 **3** Write a word with *sk*, *sw* or *str*.

1  _____

2  _____

3  _____

Workbook page 30

# Unit 4 Lesson 4

Track 33

**1** Listen and read.

**1** Some children like skating.

Oops!

Here, let's skate together.

**2** Some children like swimming in the ocean.

Come and swim with us!

**3** Some children like bowling.

She's strong!

Strike!

Hey! It's my turn.

**4** Everyone likes having friends.

Goal!

**2** Read the story again. Tick (✔) the **value**.

**Solidarity:** Play together. ☐ Play with your best friend. ☐

 **3** Read and tick (✔).

How do you feel when you are not in the game?  ☐  ☐

What can you do if someone is alone?

Invite him / her to watch your game. ☐ Invite him / her to play with you. ☐

Workbook page 31

39

# Unit 4 Lesson 5

**Track 34**

**1** Listen, point and say.

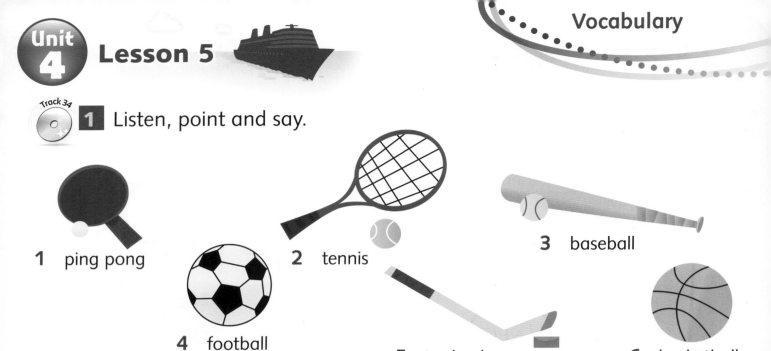

1 ping pong

2 tennis

3 baseball

4 football

5 ice hockey

6 basketball

**Track 35**

**2** Listen and guess the sports.

**3** Talk to a friend.

I like basketball.
I don't like tennis.

**Track 36**

**4** Listen and complete. Then sing. **Cool Sports**

We're smart and we play sports,
We're strong and we're athletic,
We're cool, so cool!

<u>We're playing</u> _____ .

We're smart and we play sports,
We're strong and we're athletic,
We're cool, so cool!

_____ .

We're smart and we play sports,
We're strong and we're athletic,
We're cool, so cool!

_____ .

Workbook page 32

# Lesson 6

**Grammar**

Are you / they swimming?
Yes, I am. / No, I'm not.
Yes, they are. / No, they aren't.

 Track 37

**1** Listen, read and say.

**1** Are they playing baseball?

No, they aren't. They're playing football. Look!

**2** Are you eating ice cream?

Yes, I am.

 **Discover Grammar**

Circle.

To ask a question, we use
**Are you playing? / You are playing?**
**They are skating? / Are they skating?**

**2** Look at Activity 1. Write *No, they aren't* or *Yes, they are*.

**1** Are Zac and Oona swimming? _____ .

**2** Are the boys playing football? _____ .

**3** Are they playing basketball? _____ .

 **3** Choose a sport. Play the Guessing Game.

Are you playing baseball?

Yes, I am.

# Unit 4

## Lesson 7

# Let's visit ... Italy!

**1** Read about football camps in Italy.

## Future Stars   *by Anna Totti*

Meet Giovanna Neri, a typical 9-year-old girl from Milan, Italy. Like many children in Italy, Giovanna is crazy about football. Her favourite team is AC Milan. Right now she is at a summer football camp in a town called Jesolo. Jesolo is a beautiful place by the ocean. Lots of people are at the beach sailing, swimming and surfing. Giovanna is meeting new friends at football camp and having a lot of fun. The most important part of football camp is learning to respect your companions and learning new skills.

**2** Read and answer.

1 What is Giovanna doing this summer?
2 What do you know about Jesolo?
3 Is this article positive or negative about football camps?

---

**IT'S A FACT!**

The *Azzurri* are the national football team of Italy. *Azzurri* means "the blues" – it's the colour of their strip!

---

## Think Twice

1 Do you like learning new skills? Why / Why not?
2 Why do you think sports camps are important?

**Presentation: Tell your class about a popular sport in your country.**

Template 4

**1 Prepare.**

**Find information about the sport.**
**Use the questions to help you.**

Choose a popular sport from your country.

Draw a picture and label it.

Find information about it.

Is it a team sport or an individual sport?

How many players are there?

What equipment do they use?

Is there a national team?

What are they called and why?

Why do you like this sport?

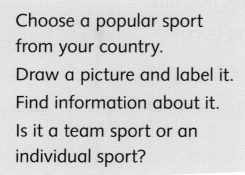

**2 Practise.**

Let me tell you about ...

I like this sport because ...

The national team is ...

There are ... players on a team.

The players wear ... and they use ...

Track 38

**3 Present.**

Hi, I'm Liam from New Zealand. Let me tell you about our national sport – it's rugby and it's really popular. The national team is the All Blacks because they wear black shirts and shorts. They play with an oval-shaped ball. There are 15 players on the team. I like this sport because it's fun to watch.

# Progress check

**Unit 4**

**TEST PREP**

**1** Choose and tick (✔) four activities. Then answer *Yes, I am* or *No, I'm not.*

eating chocolate ☐

watching TV ☐

playing a computer game ☐

riding an elephant ☐

playing ping pong ☑

skating ☐

**1** Are you playing ping pong? <u>Yes, I am</u>.

**2** Are you playing a computer game? _____.

**3** Are you eating chocolate? _____.

**4** Are you watching TV? _____.

**5** Are you skating? _____.

**6** Are you riding an elephant? _____.

/5

**2** Read and complete.

Hello Oliver!

I'm on holiday in Italy and I'm having fun. Today ¹ [ ] I <u>'m</u>

<u>swimming</u> in the ocean and ² [ ] I _____ _____ football on the

beach with my brother. ³ [✗] We _____ _____ a kite today.

My friends are here, too. ⁴ [ ] They _____ _____ ice cream,

but I don't like strawberry, so ⁵ [✗] I _____ not _____ my ice cream.

Now I'm watching two boys. ⁶ [ ] They _____ _____ .

It's a great holiday!

Bye, Vicky

/5

Total score /10

## My Progress

I can name five sports or activities.

I can say what I am doing now.

I can read and say words with *sw*, *sk* and *str*.

**44**

# Jamaica

Jamaica is beautiful!

## Zoom In

Jamaica is a hot and sunny island with beautiful beaches.

Is Jamaica in the Caribbean or in Africa?
What language do they speak in Jamaica?
What is typical weather for your country?

**Look at the picture.**
Do you think fishing is this man's hobby?

# Unit 5

## Lesson 1

 Track 39

**1** Listen, point and say.

| Sunday | Monday | Tuesday | Wednesday | Thursday | Friday | Saturday |
|--------|--------|---------|-----------|----------|--------|----------|
| sunny | cloudy | foggy | windy | hot | cold snowy | rainy |

 **2** Write and say.

**1** It isn't <u>windy</u>.
It's <u>sunny</u>.
Let's go skateboarding in the park.

**2** It isn't _____ .
It's _____ .
Let's go swimming in the ocean.

**3** It isn't _____ .
It's _____ .
Let's go skiing in the mountains.

**4** It isn't _____ .
It's _____ .
Let's go fishing in the river.

**46**

Workbook page 36

# Lesson 2

**Grammar**
What's he / she / it doing?
He's / She's / It's sleeping.
He / She / It isn't reading.

Track 40

**1** Listen, read and say.

It's hot. Zac isn't playing football. He's playing his guitar. Oona isn't reading her book. She's sleeping under a tree.

Look at the bird! It's singing. It likes Zac's song.

**Discover Grammar**

Circle.

What **is she / she is** doing?

**She's / Is she** sleeping.

**Isn't she / She isn't** swimming.

Track 41

**2** Listen and say *True* or *False*.

**3** Choose and circle. Then say.

Look at Zac. What's he doing?

**1** He's / He isn't sleeping.    **2** He's / He isn't playing his guitar.

Look at Oona. What's she doing?

**3** She's / She isn't sleeping.    **4** She's / She isn't reading.

Look at the bird. What's it doing?

**5** It's / It isn't flying.    **6** It's / It isn't singing.

Workbook page 37          Grammar Guide page 108

47

# Unit 5 Lesson 3

**1** Listen and chant.

## oo ir ow

Off to school! Where's my shirt?
And my socks and boots and skirt?

Off to the country! Look, a cow!
Flowers and trees and a big brown owl.

Off to the pool! It's really cool!
It's sunny today — I'm not going to school!

**2** Listen and complete. Then cross (✗) out the word with a different sound.

1   c __ __ l

   sch__ __ l

   fl o̲ w̲ er

   _____

2   sh __ __ t

   c __ __ l

   sk __ __ t

   _____

3   fl __ __ er

   __ __ l

   sh __ __ t

   _____

**3** Look at the pictures. Find one more word for each column.

# Unit 5 — Lesson 4

**1** Listen and read.

**1**
Kirsty is walking to school. She's wearing her skirt and her shirt, but she doesn't have her sweater.

I'm cold! I don't have my sweater.

**2**
It's rainy. Kirsty is playing in the flowers in the park. She's wearing her new shoes.

Oh, no! My new shoes! I don't have my boots.

**3**
Kirsty is at the pool. She has her sweater, her new shoes, her brown boots …

**4**
… but she can't go swimming.

Oh, no! I don't have my bathing suit!

**2** Read the story again. Tick (✔) the **value**.

**Responsibility:** Be prepared. ☐ Be kind. ☐

**3** Are you prepared and organised? Read and write *Yes* or *No*.

I make lists to help me remember. _____

I keep my bedroom neat. _____

I organise my school bag every day. _____

Workbook page 39

# Lesson 5

**Unit 5 Lesson 5** — Vocabulary

 Track 45

**1** Listen, point and say.

**1** dress

**4** jeans

**2** shorts

**3** T-shirt

**5** socks

**6** boots

 **2** Circle *True* or *False*.

| | | |
|---|---|---|
| **1** | Rosa's wearing socks. | True / False |
| **2** | She's wearing boots. | True / False |
| **3** | Rosa's wearing a dress. | True / False |
| **4** | Ben's wearing a T-shirt. | True / False |
| **5** | Ben's wearing jeans. | True / False |
| **6** | He's wearing shorts. | True / False |

Rosa          Ben

 **3** Talk to a friend about Rosa and Ben.

> Rosa's wearing a T-shirt.

> No, she's wearing a dress.

 **4** Choose a picture and play the Guessing Game. Listen and point.

> She's wearing a red skirt.

Workbook page 40

**Grammar**

Is he / she reading?
Yes, he / she is.
No, he / she isn't.

 **1** Listen, read and say.

Zac and Oona are at the train station. They're looking for Zac's friend Paul.

PLATFORM #3

Look! There's my friend.

Where? Is he wearing a hat?

No, he isn't.

Is he reading a book?

Yes, he is. Hello, Paul!

**Discover Grammar**

Circle the correct answers.

Is he riding a bike?    Yes, he is.    A bike.    He's riding a bike.    No, he isn't.

 **2** Unscramble the questions and answer them.

**1** wearing Paul Is a hat?    <u>Is Paul wearing a hat</u> ?

**2** Oona a banana? Is eating    _____ ?

**3** Paul a book? reading Is    _____ ?

 **3** Listen and complete. Then sing. **The Island Song**

It's a sunny afternoon,
On an island in the sun.
What's he doing?
He's having fun!

What's she doing?
Is she _____ a kite?
No, she isn't.
She's _____ a bike!

## Let's visit ... Jamaica!

### 1 Read a poem about Jamaica.

## Jamaica's Weather

*by Winston Miller*

Jamaica's weather,
Is great for us all!
Jamaica's weather,
Is great for us all!

It's hot and it's sunny,
And sometimes it rains.
It can be very windy,
Watch out for hurricanes!

It's hot on the beach,
But it's fresh in the pool,
And up in the mountains,
It can be a little cool!

Jamaica's weather,
Is great for us all!
Jamaica's weather,
Is great for us all!

**IT'S A FACT!**

The gold colour in the Jamaican flag represents the beautiful sunny weather in Jamaica.

### 2 Read and write.

1 Find seven weather words in the poem.
2 What's the weather like in a hurricane?
3 Does the poet like the weather in Jamaica?

## Think Twice

1 Is the weather in Jamaica great for everybody all the time? Why / Why not?
2 Think about the weather patterns in your country. Are there any problems because of the weather?

**Presentation: Tell your class about the weather in your country.**

Template 5

**1 Prepare.**

**Find information about the weather.**

- Think about the weather in your country in the different seasons.
- Draw a picture and label it.
- Find information about temperatures and weather patterns.

What is the temperature?
What is the weather like?

Is the weather the same in different parts of your country?
Do you like this time of year? Why?

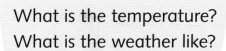

**2 Practise.**

**Describe the weather in your country.**

At the beach it's ...    In the mountains/city it's ...

Track 48
**3 Present.**

Florida

Let me tell you about the weather in Florida. It's really great. It's usually hot and sunny, especially in spring and summer. In winter it's warm, too. But the weather isn't always great. In the hurricane season sometimes it can be really windy and stormy.

# Unit 5

**1** Unscramble the verbs. Complete the sentences. Then number the pictures.

TEST PREP

1  ngis      ___sing___      He's ___singing___ a song.

2  kirdn      _____      She's _____ a fizzy drink.

3  epels      _____      The cat's _____ under the table.

4  iatpn      _____      He's _____ a picture.

5  ocok      _____      She's _____ some spaghetti.

6  tae      _____      The cat's _____ some ice cream.

/5

**2** Look and answer.

1  Is Zac playing football?      _Yes, he is_____.

2  Is Oona reading a book?      _____.

3  Is the sun shining?      _____.

4  What is the bird doing in the tree?      _____.

5  What is the boy doing in the ocean?      _____.

6  What are the two girls playing?      _____.

/5

Total score   /10

## My Progress

I can describe today's weather. ✓ ? ✗

I can say what I am wearing. ✓ ? ✗

I can read and say words with *ow*, *oo* and *ir*. ✓ ? ✗

# Chile

## Zoom In

This man lives on a farm in Chile. He's going to ride his horse to the mountains.

Is Chile near your country?
Is Chile a big country or a small country?
Can you ride a horse?

**Look at the picture.**
What is the weather like?

Welcome to Chile! Look at his horse!

# Unit 6

# Lesson 1

 **1** Listen, point and say.

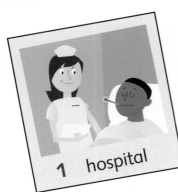

1 hospital

2 cafe

3 supermarket

4 library

5 museum

6 cinema

7 airport

8 farm

 **2** Look and write.

| 1 | 2 | 3 |
| 4 | 5 | 6 |

1 She's at the _____ .

2 He's at the _____ .

3 She's at the _____ .

4 They're at the _____ .

5 They're at the _____ .

6 He's at the _____ .

 **3** Ask and answer.

Is there a supermarket in your neighbourhood?

Yes, there is. Is there a museum in your neighbourhood?

# Unit 6 — Lesson 2

**Grammar**
Are you / we going to the cinema?
Yes, I am / we are.
No, I'm not / we aren't.

Track 3

**1** Listen, read and say.

It's 8 o'clock. Zac and Oona are going to the cinema.

5:00  7:15  9:30  11:0

Are you going to the cinema?

No, we aren't. We're going to the stadium. There's a music festival.

Now I'm going to the stadium, too!

**Discover Grammar**

Circle the correct alternatives.

Are **I / you / he / she / it / we / they** going to the park?

**2** Complete the sentences.

1
We _____ the library.
We _____ the pool.

2
They _____ the supermarket.
They _____ the airport.

**3** Think of a place. Ask and answer.

Are you going to the pool?

No, I'm not. I'm going to the museum.

# Unit 6 Lesson 3

**1** Listen to the poem.

## er    ear    ore

I'm playing with my brother.
We're very, very bored.
Let's go down to the river.
Let's go off and explore!

We're going to the river.
The water's really cool!
Let's go with our teacher
And then we'll go to school.

Now we're going to eat
Some chocolate and a pear.
An animal is watching us.
Look! A hungry bear!

**2** Find the words in the puzzle, then write.

| r | t | e | a | c | h | e | r | p | w |
|---|---|---|---|---|---|---|---|---|---|
| i | b | e | a | r | h | w | k | e | a |
| v | e | x | p | l | o | r | e | a | t |
| w | q | b | r | o | t | h | e | r | e |
| r | b | o | r | e | d | h | r | l | r |

**er**                    **ear**                    **ore**

_____        _____        _____

_____        _____        _____

_____

**3** Write one more word for each column.

_____        _____        _____

**58**

# Unit 6 Lesson 4

Track 5

**1** Listen and read.

**1**

I'm bored. Are you going to the river?

Yes, I am. Can you swim?

Yes, I can.

**2**

Look! There's a bear. Let's be careful.

Oh, I see bears all the time.

**3**

Mmm, these pears are delicious.

A bear! Quick! Jump!

**4**

Help! I can't swim!

**5**

I hate the water!

**2** Read the story again. Tick (✔) the **value**.

**Honesty:** Always be careful. ☐  Don't pretend. ☐

**3** Are you always honest? Read and write *Yes* or *No*.

1 I say what I can and can't do. _____

2 I tell the truth to my friends. _____

3 I am always honest with my parents. _____

Workbook page 47

59

# Unit 6 · Lesson 5

**Track 6**

**1** Listen, point and say.

I'm Ken. This is my family.

1 uncle

2 aunt

3 cousin

5 baby brother

4 baby sister

6 grandparents

**Track 7**

**2** Look at Activity 1. Listen and say the person.

**3** Talk to a friend about their family.

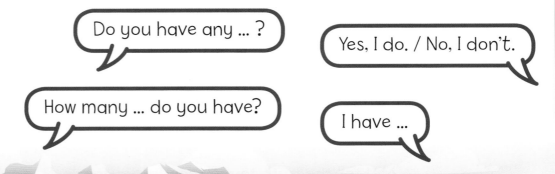

Do you have any ... ?

Yes, I do. / No, I don't.

How many ... do you have?

I have ...

# Unit 6

## Lesson 6

**Grammar**

Where's he / she going?
He's / She's going to the airport.
Is he / she going to the beach?
Yes, **he / she is.** / No, **he / she isn't.**

**Track 8**

**1** Listen, read and say.

Where's Zac going? He's going to the airport with his grandparents.

And Oona is going to the airport, too!

**Discover Grammar**

Read again. Circle.

The story is talking about **now / the future.**

**2** Complete the questions using *Where are* or *Where's*. Then answer.

1 _____ Zac going?                    _____ .

2 _____ Oona going?                   _____ .

3 _____ Zac's grandparents going?  _____ .

**Track 9**

**3** Listen, sing and act. **The Busy, Busy Song**

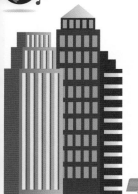

Hurry, hurry, hurry,
She's busy, busy, busy,
She's going to the library,
In the busy, busy city.

Hurry, hurry, hurry,
He's busy, busy, busy,
He's going to the stadium,
In the busy, busy city.

Workbook page 49          Grammar Guide page 108          Grammar File 6

**Lesson 7**

Unit 6

# Let's visit ... Chile!

**1** **Read about a famous glacier in Chile.**

www.kidsonholiday.com

Where can you go skiing in July, swim in the ocean in December, see penguins and llamas and eat German desserts? In Chile, of course. This long, skinny country is a very special place with many interesting places to visit.

One fantastic place is the Grey Glacier on Lake Grey in the south of Chile. Glaciers are large, frozen rivers that are usually covered in snow. They are very beautiful. Lake Grey also has icebergs! You can visit the Grey Glacier by boat and you can also go ice walking!

**IT'S A FACT!**

Almost 90 per cent of an iceberg is under water!

**2** **Read and write.**
1 What types of animals live in Chile?
2 What are glaciers made of?
3 What can you do at the glacier?

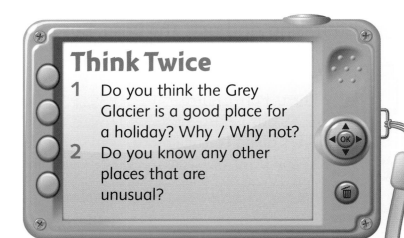

**Think Twice**
1 Do you think the Grey Glacier is a good place for a holiday? Why / Why not?
2 Do you know any other places that are unusual?

🌎 **Presentation:** **A special place in your country.**

Template 6

**1** **Prepare.**

**Find information about the place.**

- Choose a special place of natural beauty in your country.
- Draw a picture and label it.
- Find information about the place.

| Why is it special? | What can you do there? | Why do you like it? |

**2** **Practise.**

**Describe your special place.**

| Let me tell you about ... | You can ... | I like ... because ... |

Track 10

**3** **Present.**

Let me tell you about the Grand Canyon. You can travel down there on a horse or you can fly over in a plane. You can see different birds and animals there. I like it because it's really interesting.

**Unit 6**

## Progress check

**1** Choose and tick (✔) four places.
Then answer *Yes, I am* or *No, I'm not.*

|  | |  |  |  |
|-------|---|-----|----------|--------|
| the cafe | ☐ | 1 | Are you going to the mall? | Yes, I am . |
| the mall | ☑ | 2 | Are you going to the cinema? | _____ . |
| the cinema | ☐ | 3 | Are you going to the cafe? | _____ . |
| the library | ☐ | 4 | Are you going to the pool? | _____ . |
| the pool | ☐ | 5 | Are you going to the countryside? | _____ . |
| the countryside | ☐ | 6 | Are you going to the library? | _____ . |

/5

**2** Look at the picture. Answer the questions.

1  Where's the boy going?  <u>He's going to the library</u> .

2  Is the girl going to the library?  _____ .

3  Where's the woman going?  _____ .

4  Are the doctors going to the hospital?  _____ .

5  Where are the two girls going?  _____ .

6  Where are the children going?  _____ .  /5

Total score  /10

**My Progress**

I can name five places.

I can say a sentence with *I'm going to the …*

I can read and say words with *er, ear* and *ore.*

France

Look, it's the Eiffel Tower in Paris, France!

Hello, I'm Henri. I'm going to climb all 674 steps!

## Zoom In

About six million people visit the Eiffel Tower every year.

Paris is the capital of France.
What do you know about it?
What language do people speak in France?
Is there a big tower in your country?
Can you climb it?

**Look at the picture.**
Imagine Henri is at the top of the Eiffel tower.
What do you think he can see?

Unit 7

# Unit 7 Lesson 1

## Track 11

**1** Listen, point and say.

| 1 | fisherman | 3 | pilot | 5 | weight lifter | 7 | firefighter |
|---|---|---|---|---|---|---|---|
| 2 | nurse | 4 | writer | 6 | vet | 8 | police officer |

**2** Read and complete.

1 He likes flying. He works in an airport. He's a _pilot_.

2 She likes writing. She likes books. She's a _____ .

3 He's athletic and very strong. He works in a stadium. He's a _____ .

4 She works in a hospital. She's a _____ .

5 He likes the ocean. He works on a boat. He's a _____ .

6 She likes animals. She works in an animal hospital. She's a _____ .

7 He's brave and he helps people. He's a _____ .

8 She wears a uniform. She works with people and she is very responsible.

She's a _____

**3** Play the Guessing Game. Then spell.

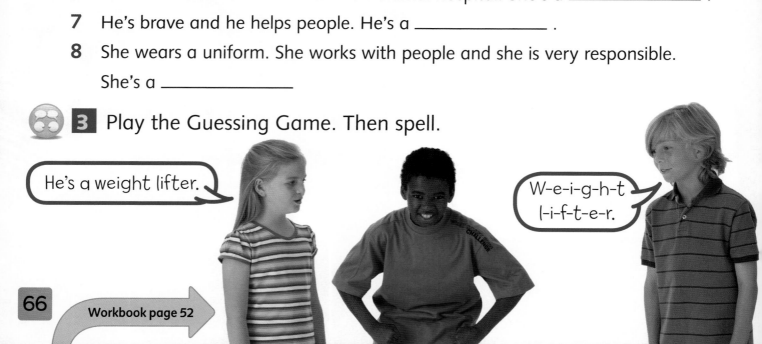

He's a weight lifter.

W-e-i-g-h-t l-i-f-t-e-r.

66

Workbook page 52

# Unit 7 — Lesson 2

**Grammar**

I'm (not) going to be a cook.
Are you going to be a pilot?
Yes, I am. / No, I'm not.

**Track 12**

**1** Listen, read and say.

**Discover Grammar**

Match.

To talk about now, we use:          I'm going to be a vet.
To talk about a future plan, we use:     I am a vet.

**2** Write two sentences about yourself. Then talk to a friend.

police officer   firefighter   nurse   vet   teacher
farmer   fisherman   weight lifter   pilot   writer

1   I'm _____ .

2   I'm not _____ .

Are you going to be a fisherman?

No, I'm not. I'm going to be a ...

# Unit 7 Lesson 3

 **1** Listen to the poem.

## ur    or    a

Cats, snakes and turtles!
My father is a vet.
He works in a world of animals,
With all kinds of pets.

My mother is a nurse.
She drives a purple car.
She works at the hospital.
It isn't very far.

I'm going to be a writer
And work with lots of words.
I'm going to write poems
About surfing, fish and birds.

 **2** Listen and complete. Then cross (✗) out the word with a different sound.

**1** f __ ther

n u r se

c __ r

_____

**2** c __ r

w __ __ k

w __ __ ld

_____

**3** n __ __ se

t __ __ tle

f __ ther

_____

 **3** Look back at the poem. Find one more word for each column.

# Unit 7 Lesson 4

**1** Listen and read.

**1**

Look at the firefighters.

What a great job! I'm going to be a firefighter.

It's a lot of work.

**2**

Look at the police officer in his fast car.

What a great job! I'm going to be a police officer.

It's a lot of work.

**3**

Look at the nurse helping the old man.

What a great job! I'm going to be a nurse.

It's a lot of work.

**4**

Dad is right. This *is* a lot of work!

**2** Read the story again. Tick (✔) the **value**.

**Effort:** Do your homework. ☐  Work hard. ☐

**3** Do you always work hard? Read and tick (✔) what you do.

1 I always try hard at school. ☐
2 I never miss a class. ☐
3 I do my homework regularly. ☐

## Unit 7 — Lesson 5

**1** Listen, point and say.

**1** do my homework

**2** take a shower

**3** call a friend

**4** use the Internet

**5** brush my teeth

**6** buy sweets

**2** Look at Activity 1. Write true sentences in your notebook. Then talk to a friend.

> I brush my teeth every day. I don't use the Internet every day.

Track 17

**3** Listen and sing. **School Days**

Monday to Friday,
Before I go to school,
I get ready in the bathroom,
What do you think I do?

Monday to Friday,
After I finish school,
I study in my bedroom,
What do you think I do?

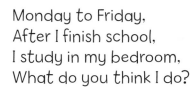

Take a shower! Brush your teeth and comb your hair!

Do your homework! Call a friend and use the Internet!

# Lesson 6

**Grammar**

He's / She's **going to** take a shower.
He / She **isn't going to** watch TV.
**Is he / she going to** play football?
Yes, **he / she is.** / No, **he / she isn't.**

Track 18

**1** Listen, read and say.

> Oona's going to brush her teeth.
> She isn't going to take a shower.

> Zac's going to take a shower.

> Oops!

💡 **Discover Grammar**

Circle the possible alternatives.
She **is / are / isn't / aren't** going to have dinner.

**2** Make sentences. Then answer the questions.

1 Zac / brush / ? / teeth _____

2 Zac / ? / take a shower _____

3 Oona / ? / brush / teeth _____

4 Oona / take a shower / ? _____

**3** Talk to a friend about what you are going to do after school today.
Then tell the class.

> watch TV    play football    make a model
> play a computer game    listen to music    read a book

> Carl is going to ...

> He isn't going to ...

**Workbook page 57**          **Grammar Guide page 109**          🖱 **Grammar File 7**          **71**

# Unit 7 — Lesson 7

## Let's visit ... France!

**1** Read about ski schools for children in France.

### Holidays in the snow

In France, skiing is very popular. In some ski resorts, there are ski schools for children. They start learning how to ski in special places called "snow gardens." They learn by playing a lot of games and having fun.

Claude Lechaume is a ski instructor. In winter, Claude works at a ski resort near a big mountain in France, called Mont Blanc. For the rest of the year, he works as a writer. The children at the ski school love Claude's lessons and they love Claude.

It's important for children to feel happy on their skis and happy on the snow.

I'm going to be a ski instructor!

I'm going to be a writer!

**IT'S A FACT!**
Children of three years old can go to ski school in France!

**2** Find and write.
1 How do children learn to ski?
2 How many jobs does Claude have?

**Think Twice**
1 Why do you think Claude's students love him?
2 Which of Claude's jobs do you think is more difficult? Why?

# Lesson 8

**Presentation: A teacher or instructor you admire.**

Template 7

**1 Prepare.**

**Find information about the person.**

- Choose a special person to talk about.
- Draw or glue pictures of him / her and add labels.
- Find information about him / her.

What does he / she teach?

Where does he / she work?

What special activities does he / she do?

Who are his / her students?

Why do you admire this teacher / instructor?

**2 Practise.**

**Describe your special person.**

Let me tell you about ...

He / She works ...

His / Her lessons are ...

His / Her students are ...

I admire him / her because ...

Track 19

**3 Present.**

Let me tell you about my football coach. His name is Rick. He works at the community centre and his lessons are great. We all want to learn his football skills. I admire him because he is a good teacher and he's a fantastic football player.

## Unit 7

**1** Look at the pictures and write.

**1** football player **2** nurse **3** vet **4** pilot **5** firefighter **6** police officer

**1** <u>He's going to be a football player</u> .   **4** _____ .

**2** _____ .   **5** _____ .

**3** _____ .   **6** _____ .

/5

**2** Look at the pictures and complete the words in the story.

Today, I'm not going to school – it's Saturday! First ¹  <u>I'm going to take a</u>

<u>shower </u>and then ²  _____ .

This morning, I'm going to ³ 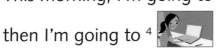 _____ and

then I'm going to ⁴  _____ .

This afternoon, I'm not going to ⁵ _____ ,

it's finished! I'm going to ⁶ _____ .

/5

Total score    /10

### My Progress

I can name five jobs.   ✓ ? ✗

I can say sentences with *I'm going to be* …   ✓ ? ✗

I can read and say words with *ur, or* and *a*.   ✓ ? ✗

METRO

I'm Lucy Hill and I was born in the USA.

We're in the USA. It's Independence Day.

## Zoom In

Independence Day is on the fourth of July.

What is the capital city of the USA?
Do you know how many states there are? How many can you name?
Do you have parades in your country? When?

**Look at the picture.**
What is happening in Lucy's city today?

Unit 8

# Unit 8 Lesson 1

**1** Listen, point and say. Then ask and answer.

| | | |
|---|---|---|
| 1. January | 2. February | 3. March |
| 4. April | 5. May | 6. June |
| 7. July<br>Oona's Birthday | 8. August | 9. September |
| 10. October | 11. November | 12. December |

When's your birthday?

My birthday's in July.

**2** Listen and say what's next.

**3** Find out and complete the birthday chart.

1 When's your teacher's birthday?  3 When's your mum's birthday?

2 When's your best friend's birthday?  4 When's your birthday?

**Lesson 2**

**Grammar**

I was / They were born in a hospital / March.
Were you born in January?
Yes, I was. / No, I wasn't.
Were they born in June?
Yes, they were. / No, they weren't.

**1** Listen, read and say.

They're cute! They're really small.

Were they born in a hospital?

No, I wasn't. I was born at home.

Thanks! They were born in February.

Yes, they were. Were you born in a hospital, too?

And I was born in a jungle!

 **Discover Grammar**

Circle.

| I | was / were | |
|---|---|---|
| You | was / were | born. |
| They | was / were | |

**2** Look at Activity 1. Circle *Yes* or *No*.

1 Were the babies born in August? Yes / No
2 Were they born in February? Yes / No
3 Were they born in a hospital? Yes / No

 **3** Talk to a friend.

1 When were you born?
2 Were you born in a hospital?
3 Were you born at home?

When were you born?

I was born in ...

Workbook page 61          Grammar Guide page 109

77

# Unit 8 — Lesson 3

**1** Listen to the poem.

## dr   ld   gr

My grandpa's really great
And he's very, very old.
He has an old green coat,
He wears it when it's cold.

He drives an old green car
When he comes to visit me.
He tells me lots of stories,
And drinks a cup of tea.

**2** Circle the words, then sort and write.

grandpadrinkdrivecoldgreenold

| **dr** | **ld** | **gr** |
|---|---|---|
| _____ | _____ | _____ |
| _____ | _____ | _____ |

**3** Write a word with *dr*, *ld* or *gr*.

1          2          3

_____    _____    _____

78

Workbook page 62

# Unit 8 Lesson 4

Track 24

**1** Listen and read.

1

It's very green here. There are lots of sheep.

Hey! Sheep don't like drinking fizzy drinks. Don't drop litter!

2

There are lots of cows here.

There's an old bull, too! Close the gate! Run!

3

Ouch!

Don't pick wild flowers. They're important for bees.

4

Now, please remember, respect the environment.

We know, Grandpa. Don't drop litter, close the gates and don't pick wild flowers.

**2** Read the story again. Tick (✔) the **value**.

**Respect:** Respect the environment. ☐ Don't drop litter. ☐

**3** Do you respect the environment? Circle what you do.

I never drop litter. / I don't pick wild flowers. / I respect animals.

Workbook page 63

79

# Unit 8  Lesson 5

**1** Listen, point and say.

**1**  happy

**2**  sad

**3**  tired

**4**  bored

**5**  excited

**6**  scared

**7**  mad

**2** Listen and act.

**3** Listen and complete. Then sing. **In Your Dreams**

Last night, in your dreams,
Were you big?
Were you small?

Were you _____ ?

Were you _____ ?

Last night, in your dreams,
Were you happy?

Were you _____ ?
Were you tired?

Were you _____ ?

## Lesson 6

**Grammar**
You / They **were** at an airport.
You / They **weren't** happy.

 Track 28

**1** Listen, read and say.

Look at my grandparents! They were pilots! They were at an airport.

Look, Zac! You were very small. You weren't very happy!

1974    2006

**Discover Grammar**

Circle.

They were(n't) sad tells us **about now / yesterday.**

You are(n't) tired tells us **about now / yesterday.**

**2** Look at Activity 1. Circle the correct words.

| | | | |
|---|---|---|---|
| **1** | In 1974, Zac's grandparents | were / weren't | at an airport. |
| **2** | In 1974, Zac's grandparents | were / weren't | teachers. |
| **3** | In 2006, Zac | was / wasn't | small. |
| **4** | In 2006, Zac | was / wasn't | young. |

**3** Look around your classroom. Act it out and say.

You were in front of the board.

# Let's visit ... the USA!

## 1 Read about film stars in the USA.

www.film-stars.com

The USA is the home of the movies and lots of movie stars live and work in Hollywood, California. Many actors are very talented – they can act happy or sad, friendly or mad, excited or bored.

The most important award for an actor is the famous Oscar®. Every year, there is an awards ceremony in February or March. There's also a road in Hollywood called the Hollywood Walk of Fame, where many famous people have "stars" on the sidewalk. Some movie stars make prints of their hands and feet in front of a famous theatre.

### IT'S A FACT!

The youngest person to win an acting Oscar was Tatum O'Neal. She was ten!

## 2 Read and write.

1 What emotions can actors act?
2 Where do famous actors make hand and footprints?

### Think Twice

1 Who is your favourite movie star? Why do you like him / her?
2 Do you think awards are important for actors? Why? / Why not?

## Presentation: A famous actor.

Template 8

### 1 Prepare.

**Find information about the person.**

- Choose a special person to talk about.
- Draw or glue pictures of him / her, and label them.
- Find information about him / her.

| Where is he / she from? | Where does he / she work? |
|---|---|

Can you name a film he / she is in?  Who does he / she play?

What emotions does he / she use in the film?  Do you like this actor?

### 2 Practise.

**Describe your person.**

Let me tell you about ...  He / She is from ...  He / She works in ...

He / She is in the film ... and he / she acts ...

I like / don't like ... because ...

Track 29

### 3 Present.

Let me tell you about my favourite movie star. His name is Johnny Depp and he's from the USA. He works in Hollywood making movies. He's in the *Pirates of the Caribbean* movies and he acts the part of Captain Jack Sparrow. I like him because he's funny.

**Unit 8**

**TEST PREP**

**1** Complete the months. Then write answers for you.

1 Were you born in M <u>a</u> <u>y</u> ?                     <u>No, I wasn't</u> .

2 Were you at school in O _ t _ b _ r?                     _____ .

3 Was your teacher at school in J _ _ y?                     _____ .

4 Were your friends in the mountains in F _ _ _ u _ _ y?     _____ .

/6

**2** Read. Then choose and write the correct word.

1 Yesterday was my birthday. I was very ___<u>happy</u>___ because it was my party.

2 But my friend Pete was _____ because there wasn't any cake.

3 My mum was _____ because the house was messy.

4 The party was great – lots of games and we weren't _____ .

5 At the end, we were very _____ and sleepy.

| 1 a happy | b sad | c tired |
| 2 a happy | b tired | c sad |
| 3 a mad | b excited | c happy |

| 4 a excited | b scared | c bored |
| 5 a mad | b bored | c tired |

/4

Total score /10

**My Progress**

I can name five months of the year.     ✓ ? ✗
I can say how I was feeling.             ✓ ? ✗
I can say when I was born.               ✓ ? ✗

# Morocco

We're in Morocco! It's fascinating here!

## Zoom In

Morocco is a very hot country near the Sahara Desert. There are lots of colourful markets in Morocco.

Which continent is Morocco in? Can you find it on a map?

How many languages do they speak in Morocco?

Do you have any markets like this in your country?

**Look at the picture.**
What food can you buy?

# Unit 9

# Unit 9 Lesson 1

Track 30

**1** Listen, point and say.

1
seven thirty

2
a quarter past ten

3
a quarter to three

4
🌙 midnight

5
☀ noon

Track 31

**2** Listen and draw the times on the clocks. Then write.

1    I was at the club at
_____ .

2    I was at the library
at _____ .

3    I was at the pool at
_____ .

4    I was in bed at
_____ .

**3** Choose a time and talk to a friend.

Eight thirty!

I was at school.

86    Workbook page 68

# Unit 9 · Lesson 2

**Grammar**  I / He / She **was** in the city.
I / He / She **wasn't** at the flower market.

**1** Listen, read and say.

At a quarter past nine yesterday morning, Oona and Zac were in the city. Zac was at the flower market. Oona wasn't at the flower market. She was at the fruit market.

At a quarter to eleven, they were on the bus.

Look! I was at the flower market.

I wasn't at the flower market. I was at the fruit market ...

  **Discover Grammar**

Circle the correct alternatives.

Yesterday, **I / you / he / she / it / we / they** was in the park.

**2** Circle *True* or *False*.

1 At a quarter to nine, Zac was at the flower market.   True / False
2 At a quarter past nine, Zac was at the flower market.   True / False
3 At a quarter past nine, Oona was at the fruit market.   True / False
4 At ten o'clock, they were on the bus.   True / False

 **3** Talk about yourself.

Yesterday afternoon, at two thirty, I was ... / I wasn't ...

Yesterday evening, at a quarter past eight, I was ... / I wasn't ...

# Unit 9 Lesson 3

Track 33

**1** Listen and chant.

## air   ou   oy

I have fair hair and a pair of blue eyes.

I can shout with my mouth — shout out loud!

This boy, Roy, is playing with his toys.

Track 34

**2** Listen and complete. Then cross (✘) out the word with a different sound.

**1** h a _i_ _r_

b __ __

t __ __

_____

**2** m __ __ t h

t __ __

s h __ __ t

_____

**3** p __ __ r

h __ __ r

m __ __ t h

_____

**3** Look back at the chant. Find one more word for each column.

Workbook page 70

# Unit 9 Lesson 4

**1** Listen and read.

**2** Read the story again. Tick (✔) the **value**.

**Responsibility:** Follow the example of others. ☐  Set a good example. ☐

**3** What do you do to set a good example? Read and tick (✔).

I am on time for school. ☐  I clean my room. ☐

I do my homework. ☐  I am polite to everyone. ☐

# Unit 9 Lesson 5

**1** Listen, point and say.

Monday   Tuesday   Wednesday   Thursday   Friday

1 picnic
2 birthday party
3 wedding
4 barbecue
5 parade

**2** Remember and circle *True* or *False*.

| | | |
|---|---|---|
| 1 | They were at a wedding on Wednesday. | (True) / False |
| 2 | They were at a birthday party on Tuesday. | True / False |
| 3 | They were at a barbecue on Friday. | True / False |
| 4 | They were at a parade on Monday. | True / False |
| 5 | They were at a picnic on Wednesday. | True / False |

**3** Draw a picture of an event you were at last year. Then play a guessing game.

Were you at a barbecue?

No, I wasn't.

Were you at a wedding?

Yes, I was.

# Unit 9  Lesson 6

**Grammar**

Was he / she / it at a barbecue?
Yes, he / she / it was.
No, he / she / it wasn't.

**1** Listen, read and say.

**Match the three columns**

| | | |
|---|---|---|
| In a statement with *be* we use | subject + verb | **Was he / she … ?** |
| In a question with *be* we use | verb + subject | **He / She was …** |

**2** Look at Activity 1. Ask and answer.

**3** Listen and complete. Then sing. **The Mystery Song**

_____ he at a barbecue?          He _____ at a barbecue,

_____ she at the zoo?          She _____ at the zoo.

Where *were* they?          Where _____ they?

_____ they with you?          They _____ with you!

# Unit 9 — Lesson 7

## Let's visit ... **Morocco!**

### 1 Read about a wedding in Morocco.

Afdal's sister was beautiful in her traditional dress and jewels. Her hands and feet were painted in henna with special designs for good luck.

There was music and singing and dancing all night and there were many visitors from different villages. It was very exciting for Afdal!

Yesterday was a special day for 10-year-old Afdal Eddine. It was his sister's wedding day. Weddings are very special in Morocco.

Before the ceremony, there was a team of chefs to prepare delicious meals for family members and friends. There were more than 100 guests at the wedding.

**IT'S A FACT!**

Some Moroccan weddings take place over three days!

### 2 Read and write.

1 What happened during the wedding?
2 Can you describe Afdal's sister on her wedding day?

**Think Twice**

1 Do you know any other ceremonies with singing and dancing?
2 Are weddings similar in your country?

🌎 **Presentation: A special ceremony in your country.**

**1 Prepare.**

**Find information about the ceremony.**

- Choose a special ceremony to talk about.
- Draw or glue pictures of it and add labels.
- Find information about it.

What happens before the ceremony?

What kind of food do people eat?

How many people attend the ceremony?

What do people wear?

What do people do?

**2 Practise.**

**Describe your ceremony.**

Let me tell you about ...     Normally, ... people attend the ceremony

People eat ...          ... wear(s) ...          People ...

Track 39

**3 Present.**

Graduation
Cake

Let me tell you about our school graduation ceremony. Normally, about 200 people attend the ceremony. The boys wear suits and the girls wear dresses. The parents watch and the teachers present pieces of paper called degrees. After the ceremony, people have big parties.

**Unit 9**

**TEST PREP**

**1** Look at the pictures and read the story. Then answer the questions.

Monday     Wednesday     Friday     Saturday     Sunday

Andy was very busy this week. On Monday, he was at a picnic with his friend Jamie. On Wednesday, he was at the holiday parade. On Friday Andy was at his birthday party with all his friends. On Saturday Andy and his sister were at their cousin's wedding. On Sunday Andy was at a family barbecue. Yummy!

1 Was Andy at a wedding on Monday? _No, he wasn't. He was at a picnic_ .

2 Was he at a party on Wednesday? _____ .

3 Where was Andy on his birthday? _____ .

4 Where was Andy on Saturday? _____ .

5 Was Jamie at the barbecue with Andy? _____ .

What is the best name for this story? Tick (✔) one box.

Andy's birthday party ☐   Andy's holiday ☐   Andy's busy week ☐

/5

**2** Now write answers for you.

1 Were you at school at 9 o'clock today? _____ .

2 Were you at home yesterday at 4 o'clock? _____ .

3 Were you at a party on Saturday? _____ .

4 Was your best friend at your birthday party? _____ .

5 Was your teacher at school on Sunday? _____ .

/5

Total score /10

**My Progress**

I can name three events.   ✔ ? ✘

I can talk about an event I was at.   ✔ ? ✘

I can ask questions with *Was / Were* … ?   ✔ ? ✘

Vietnam

I'm in Vietnam. Look at his hat!

# Zoom In

The boy is from Vietnam. He's wearing a traditional hat to protect him from the sun and the rain.

Which countries are next to Vietnam on a map?

What is the weather like in Vietnam?

Do you have traditional clothes in your country? What are they?

**Look at the picture.** Where do you think the boy is?

Unit 10

# Lesson 1

 Track 40

**1** Listen, point and say.

1 furniture
2 toys
3 animals
4 food
5 money
6 clothes

 Track 41

**2** Listen and say *It's* or *They're* …

**3** Label the groups and complete with words from the box.

| ~~pounds~~ | chair | ball | T-shirt | cat | sandwich |
| pence | table | turtle | trousers | robot | apple |

| money | | |
| --- | --- | --- |
| _pounds_ | | |
| _____ | _____ | _____ |

| | | |
| --- | --- | --- |
| _____ | _____ | _____ |
| _____ | _____ | _____ |

**Grammar**

**There was some** furniture.
**There was a** horse.
**There were some** flowers.

**1** Listen, read and say.

**1**

This morning, Zac was at a parade.

**2**

Where were you this morning, Zac?

I was at the parade. It was fun! There were some animals and there was a horse! There was some food, too.

**Discover Grammar**

Circle.

We use **there was / there were** to talk about one thing.

We use **there was / there were** to talk about two or more things.

We use **there was / there were** to talk about things we can't count.

**2** Complete the sentences.

1 ___There were___ some flags.

2 _____ a horse.

3 _____ some food.

4 _____ some flowers.

**3** Play a memory game.

There were three pencils. There was some money. And there was one ruler.

# Unit 10

## Lesson 3

**Track 43**

**1** Listen to the poem.

**sm    sc    tr**

I'm a sailor on the seas,
And I'm travelling for pleasure.
I can see a small island,
Maybe there's some treasure!

Now I'm on the island,
It's scary and it's still.
I see trees, birds and fruit,
But I'm hungry and ill.

There's some smoke in the trees.
I think I see a house,
Wait! I hear an animal.
A scorpion? No, a mouse!

**2** Circle, sort and write.

scaredtreesmallscorpionsmoketravel

| sm | sc | tr |
|---|---|---|
| _____ | _____ | _____ |
| _____ | _____ | _____ |

**3** Write a word with *sm*, *sc* or *tr*.

_____        _____        _____

98

# Unit 10  Lesson 4

**1** Listen and read.

**1**

Look! A small island. We can try here!

**2** In July, the sailors were happy. There was food for everyone. There were fish in the ocean and there was fruit on the trees.

**3** But in January, there wasn't any food. The sailors were hungry and scared.

What are we going to eat?

I don't know.

**4** Some natives were nearby.

We have some food.

Let's help them.

**5** They were generous and they were friendly. And there was food for everyone again.

You are true friends.

**6** Now the sailors weren't hungry or scared. They were happy.

Smile, please.

**2** Read the story again. Tick (✔) the **value**.

**Solidarity:** Help those in need. ☐  Help your friends. ☐

**3** Do you help those in need? Read and write *Yes* or *No*.

I help my family. _____  I visit friends if they are sick. _____

I share my food with hungry people. _____

 Track 45

**1** Listen, point and say.

**1** spring

**2** summer

**3** autumn

**4** winter

**5** snow

**6** ice

**7** water

 **2** Circle and say.

| | | |
|---|---|---|
| 1 | Ice is | hot. / cold. |
| 2 | Snow is | hot. / cold. |
| 3 | People can ski in | the winter. / the summer. |
| 4 | Fish can swim in | snow. / water. |

**3** Write about the weather in your city. Then talk to a friend.

**1** Is it cold in winter?                    _____ .

**2** Is it rainy in summer?                   _____ .

**3** In winter, is there any ice on the rivers?     _____ .

**4** In spring, is there any snow?            _____ .

**5** In autumn, are there leaves on the pavement?   _____ .

Is it cold in winter?

# Unit 10 — Lesson 6

**Grammar** How much food **was there?**
How many children **were there?**

**1 Listen, read and say.**

> I was at a great party last night.

> How much food was there?

> There was lots of food.

> How many children were there?

> There weren't any children, but there were lots of animals!

**Discover Grammar**

Circle.

We use **how much / how many** to ask about things we can count.
We use **how much / how many** to ask about things we can't count.

**2 Listen and complete. Then sing. Last Summer**

Last summer ...

How _____ water _____ _____ in the pool?
There was lots. There was lots and lots.

How _____ children _____ _____ at school?
There weren't any. There weren't any at all.

Last spring ...

How _____ leaves _____ _____ on the trees?
There were lots. There were lots and lots.

How _____ ice _____ _____ in the pool?
There wasn't any. There wasn't any at all.

**Workbook page 81** | **Grammar Guide page 110** | **Grammar File 10**

101

# Let's visit ... Vietnam!

**1** Read about water puppets in Vietnam.

www.water-puppets.com

Hello friends,

This week, I want to tell you about a very original kind of theatre in my country. Vietnam is a very rainy place — it rains in winter, spring, summer and autumn. Water is very important in Vietnam. There are lots of rivers and rice paddy fields and there is a lot of water everywhere. More than a thousand years ago, rice farmers were in the fields all day. For entertainment, they invented water puppets. Water puppet shows are stories about everyday life in Vietnamese villages. They are very funny! Today, there are water puppet shows in special theatres. My favourite characters are the animals and dragons. The audience can get very wet at a water puppet show!

**IT'S A FACT!**

Sometimes the dragon puppets can look like they are breathing fire!

**2** Read and write.
1  When does it rain in Vietnam?
2  What do you find out about water puppet shows?

## Think Twice
1  Do you think water puppet shows are fun? Why?
2  Are there any traditional puppet shows in your country? Describe them.

## Presentation: A traditional show from your country.

www.
Template 10

### 1 Prepare.

**Find information about the show.**

- Choose a special type of show to talk about.
- Draw or glue pictures of it and add labels.
- Find information about it.

What part of your country is it from?
How old is it?
Where is it performed?

What kind of characters are there?
Do you like this kind of show / performance? Why? / Why not?

### 2 Practise.

**Describe your ceremony.**

Let me tell you about ...    It's performed in ...    Characters are ...

It's from ...    I like / don't like ... because ...

Track 48

### 3 Present.

Let me tell you about a traditional puppet show in Turkey. It's performed in the villages, but originally it was from a city called Bursa. Typical characters are men and animals. I like it because it's fun.

**Unit 10**

**TEST PREP**

**1** Unscramble the words. Then write sentences.

1  syto          _There were some toys_          .

2  tunrfeuir     _There was some furniture_       .

3  nemoy         _____ .

4  minalas       _____ .

5  selothc       _____ .

6  ofod          _____ .

/4

**2** Sort the words into two lists.

water    eggs    bread    bananas    nurses    sausages    snow
parties    soup    chocolate    cupcakes    ice    grapes    milk

**How much**              **How many**

____water____            ____bananas____

_____         _____

_____         _____

_____         _____

_____         _____

_____         _____

_____         _____

/6

Total score    /10

**My Progress**

I can make sentences with *There was / were* …

I can answer questions with: *How many* … ?

I can read and say words with *sm, sc* and *tr.*

Workbook page 83

# How to use the Grammar Guide

Hello! I'm Gabi! I'm your Grammar Guide for this level. I love grammar! Grammar is great and grammar is easy! I'm here to help you with all the grammar in your book. Come and visit me after each grammar lesson!

## Gabi's Home Study Guide

1 Read your Grammar Guide again at home.
2 Look at the example. Close your book. Try to say the example.
3 Open your book and check.
4 Make new examples to practise.

**1** After your grammar lesson, turn to the Grammar Guide. Look at the example.

Let's go **to** the zoo!
Let's go **by** train.

**2** Complete the activity. Use the example to help you.
Complete the sentences.
1 _____ bike.
2 _____ the park.
3 _____ the desert.
4 _____ plane.
5 _____ car.

**3** Check your answers and then colour the passport stamp.

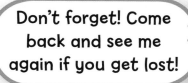

Don't forget! Come back and see me again if you get lost!

# Unit 1

## Lesson 2

**Let's go to** the zoo!
**Let's go by** train.

**Complete the sentences.**

1 _____ bike.

2 _____ the park.

3 _____ the desert.

4 _____ plane.

5 _____ car.

## Lesson 6

The park is **next to** the castle.
The city is **in front of** the pyramid.
The pyramid is **behind** the city.

**Complete the sentences with one word.**

1 The city is _____ to the ocean.

2 The jungle is _____ the city.

3 The city is in _____ of the jungle.

4 The ocean is next _____ the city.

5 The jungle isn't _____ front of the city.

# Unit 2

## Lesson 2

**There are some** eggs.
**There aren't any** grapes.

**Complete the sentences.**

1 There aren't _____ pears.

2 _____ are some sausages.

3 _____ are _____ cherries.

4 There _____ any biscuits.

5 _____ aren't _____ cupcakes.

## Lesson 6

**There's some** bread.
**There isn't any** soup.

**Is there any** cheese?
Yes, **there is**. / No, **there isn't**.

**Match.**

1 There's
2 There isn't
3 Is there
4 There's some
5 Yes,
6 No,

a any bread.
b any soup?
c there isn't.
d chocolate.
e some milk.
f there is.

# Unit 3

## Lesson 2

> **Where are you from?**
> **I'm from** Spain. / **I'm** Spanish.
>
> **Where's he / she from?**
> **He's / She's from** Spain.
> **He's / She's** Spanish.

**Complete the sentences.**

1 _____ he _____? _____ from Turkey.

2 He's _____ Japan. _____ Japanese.

3 Where's _____ _____? She's _____ South Korea.

4 Where _____ you _____? I'm from _____.

## Lesson 6

> Sing with **me / us / them / him / her.**
> Let's sing with **him / her / them.**
> Can I help **you**?
> Climb **it / them.**

**Circle.**

1 Open <u>the window</u>, please. it / me

2 Can you help <u>my sister and me</u>, please? you / us

3 Peter is with <u>Gabi</u>. him / her

4 Can I write to <u>Peter and Gabi</u>? them / you

5 I like <u>strawberries</u>. them / us

# Unit 4

## Lesson 2

> **I'm sailing.** | **We're** playing.
> **I'm not** fishing. | **We aren't** swimming.

**Complete the sentences.**

1 (We / not / fish) _____ at the beach.
(We / surf) _____ in the ocean.

2 (I / not / skate) _____ at the park.
(I / ski) _____ in the mountains.

3 (We / dive) _____ in the pool.
(We / not / sail) _____ at the beach.

4 (I / not / climb) _____ in the mountains.
(I / walk) _____ in the jungle.

## Lesson 6

> **Are you** playing baseball?
> Yes, **I am.** / No, **I'm not.**
> **Are they** playing baseball?
> Yes, **they are.** / No, **they aren't.**

**Complete the sentences.**

1 _____ they running? Yes, they _____.

2 Are _____ eating? No, I'm _____.

3 _____ they talking? No, they _____.

4 _____ you writing? Yes, _____ _____.

## Unit 5

### Lesson 2

> **What's he / she / it doing?**
> **He's / She's / It's eating** a banana.
> **He isn't / She isn't / It isn't eating** a sandwich.

**Complete the sentences.**

1 _____ the monkey _____?

2 What's Gabi _____? _____ sleeping.

3 _____ the bird _____? _____ singing.

4 Zac _____ reading a book. _____ writing.

### Lesson 6

> **Is he / she** wearing a hat?
> Yes **he /she is. /** No **he / she isn't.**

**Complete the questions and answers.**

1 (he / wear) _____ a skirt?
No, _____ _____.

2 (she / eat) _____ a banana? Yes, _____ _____.

3 (Paul / read) _____ a book?
_____, _____ isn't.

4 (Gabi / ride) _____ a bike?
_____, _____ is.

## Unit 6

### Lesson 2

> **Where are you going?**
> **Are you going to** the library?
> No, **I'm not. I'm going to** the cinema.
>
> **Are you going to** the cinema? Yes, **I am!**
> **They are going to** the cinema.

**Match.**

| | | |
|---|---|---|
| 1 Where | a | you going to the pool? |
| 2 Are | b | I'm not. |
| 3 No, | c | I am. |
| 4 They | d | are they going? |
| 5 Yes, | e | are going to the museum. |

### Lesson 6

> **Where is he going?**
> **He's going to** the stadium.
>
> **Is she going to** the stadium, too?
> No, **she isn't.**

**Complete the sentences.**

1 _____ is she going?

2 _____ he going _____ the pool?
No, _____ _____.

3 Is _____ _____ to _____ stadium?
_____, he is.

4 Where is _____ _____?

# Unit 7

## Lesson 2

> **Are you going to be** a police officer?
> No, **I'm not. I'm going to be** a vet.
> **Are you going to be** a vet?
> Yes, **I am!**

**Complete the sentences.**

1 _____ you going to _____ a nurse?
_____, I am.

2 Are you _____ _____ be a teacher?
_____, _____ not.

3 I'm going _____ _____ _____ writer.

## Lesson 6

> On Saturday **he / she's going to** take a shower.
> **He / She isn't going to** play football.
> **Is he / she going to** watch TV on Saturday?
> **Yes, he / she is.**
> **Is he / she going to** use the internet?
> **No, he / she isn't.**

**Match.**

1 He's          a isn't going to watch TV.
2 She           b he is.
3 Is            c going to play football.
4 Yes,          d he going to read a book?
5 No,           e she isn't.

# Unit 8

## Lesson 2

> **I was born** in a hospital.
> **Were you born in** March?
> **No, I wasn't. / Yes, I was!**
> **Were they born in** March?
> **Yes, they were. / No, they weren't.**

**Complete the sentences.**

1 _____ you born _____ August? No, I
_____.

2 I _____ born _____ April.
I was _____ in March.

3 Were _____ born _____ a hospital?
Yes, they _____.

## Lesson 6

> **You were** at the beach yesterday. **You weren't** at school.
> **They were** at the airport. **They weren't** at home.

**Unscramble and write the sentences.**

1 at yesterday home weren't You

_____.

2 were the You stadium at

_____.

3 grandparents weren't Gabi's teachers

_____.

## Unit 9

### Lesson 2

I / He / She was at the flower market yesterday.
I / He / She wasn't at the mall.

**Write was / wasn't.**

1 Gabi _____ at the flower market yesterday.

2 She _____ with her friends.

3 She _____ with her parents.

### Lesson 6

Was he / she at the party?
Yes, he /she was. / No, he / she wasn't.
Was the cat at the party?
Yes, it was. / No, it wasn't.

**Complete the sentences.**

1 _____ it rainy yesterday?
No, _____ _____.

2 _____ your sister at the party?
Yes, _____ _____.

3 _____ the party fun?
Yes, _____ _____.

4 Where _____ John yesterday?
_____ was at the zoo.

## Unit 10

### Lesson 2

There was some food.
There was a horse.
There were some elephants.

**Circle the correct words.**

1 There was / were a / some animals.

2 There was / were a / some food.

3 There was / were a / some flag.

4 There was / were one / some horse.

5 There was / were a / three elephants.

### Lesson 6

How much water was there?
There was lots. / There wasn't any.
How many trees were there?
There were lots. / There weren't any.

**Complete the sentences.**

1 How _____ flowers _____ there?
_____ _____ lots.

2 _____ _____ children were _____? There _____ any.

3 _____ _____ leaves _____ _____? _____ were lots.

4 _____ _____ ice _____ _____ ? _____ _____ any.

Macmillan Education Limited
4 Crinan Street, London N1 9XW

Companies and representatives throughout the world

ISBN 978-0-230-46644-9

Concept design by Macmillan Education Limited, Ben Cracknell Studios and Deb Oatley at room9design
Page make-up by Ben Cracknell Studios and Deb Oatley at room9design
Illustrated by Gabriele Antonini (Advocate Art) pp9, 19, 29, 39, 49, 59, 69, 79, 89, 99; Fiona Gowen pp14, 18, 24, 29, 38, 44, 46, 49, 74, 78; Anna Hancock (Beehive) pp8, 18, 28, 38, 48, 58, 68, 78, 88, 98; David Hurtado pp8, 18, 21, 28, 34, 38, 38, 44, 48, 54, 58, 64, 68, 70, 78, 84, 88, 98, 105, 106, 107, 108, 109, 110; Gerald Kelly pp3, 4, 5, 6, 7, 11, 12, 13, 15, 17, 21, 22, 23, 25, 27, 31, 32, 33, 37, 41, 42, 43, 47, 51, 52, 53, 57, 61, 62, 63, 67, 71, 72, 73, 76, 77, 81, 82, 83, 87, 91, 92, 93, 97, 101, 102, 103; Rob McClurkan pp10, 16, 26, 30, 36, 40, 46, 50, 56, 60, 66, 70, 76, 80, 86, 90, 96, 100; Mark Ruffle (The Organisation) pp7, 14, 20, 21, 24, 31, 34, 37, 44, 51, 54, 57, 61, 64, 74, 84, 91, 94, 101, 104.
Cover design by Macmillan Education Limited
Cover illustration by Pablo Scapinachis – Arquiplay
Cover photography by Alamy/Woodbridge Aviation Images (plane), Studio8 (child)
Picture research by Emily Taylor

The authors and publishers would like to thank the following for permission to reproduce their photographs:

**Alamy**/Arco Images GmbH p13(t), Alamy/Jon Arnold Images Ltd p35, Alamy/Kevin Foy p92(b), Alamy/Gemstone Images p43(boy), Alamy/Robert Harding Picture Library p63(bl), Alamy/Martin Harvey p62(c), Alamy/Hemis pp5, 83, Alamy/Imagebroker p102(c), Alamy/Images & Stories p103(b), Alamy/Look Die Bilderagentur der Fotografen GmbH p45, Alamy/Mediablitzimages(uk) p23(t), Alamy/Kadar Meguedad p64, Alamy/Renee Morris p12(t), Alamy/Stock Connection Blue p13(c), Alamy/Travel Pictures p94, Alamy/World Pictures p103(t); **Corbis**/Ausloeser/Zefa p73(t), Corbis/Adie Bush p72(man), Corbis/Ralph A Clevenger p62(b), Corbis/David Cumming/Eye Ubiquitous p52(c), Corbis/Peter M Fisher p27(b); Corbis/Free Agents Limited p102(t), Corbis/KidStock/Blend Images p75, Corbis/John Gress/Reuters p84(br), Corbis/Frans Lemmens p92(c), Corbis/Ian Lishman/Juice Images p72(girl), Corbis/Helios Loo p32(t), Corbis/Chris Karges p72(boy), Corbis/MM Productions pp43(b), 73(c), Corbis/Picture Net p52(b), Corbis/Bertrand Rieger/Hemis p72(t), Corbis/Patrick Robert/Sygma p22(c), Corbis/Gavin Wickham/Eye Ubiquitous p52(t); **FLPA**/Mitsuaki Iwago/Minden Pictures p63(c), FLPA/Frans Lanting p15; **Getty**/AFP p25, Getty/Age fotostock p55, Getty/Walter Bibikow, Getty/James P Blair p53(b), Getty/Rob Brimson p93(t), Getty/Daniel J Cox p13(b), Getty/Flickr/Crawford A. Wilson III p52(t), Getty/David Deas p52(cr), Getty/Garry Gay pp22(b), 23(c, b), Getty/John Giustina p42(t), Getty/William J Hebert p62(t), Getty/Jon Kopaloff p82(t), Getty/Pascal Le Segretain p82(b), Getty/Eamonn McCormack p83(t), Getty/Joseph Sohm-Visions of America p32(b), Getty/WireImage p83(c), Getty/National Geographic/Stephen St John p33(c), Getty/Christopher Pillitz p27(t), Getty/Heath Robbins p12(b), Getty/David Sanger p33(b), Getty/Stockbyte pp33(t), 42(b); **Macmillan Education Ltd**/Paul Bricknell pp11, 13(boy), 33(girl), 37, 41, 53(b), 63(br), 66(bx3), 73(b), 81, 83(b), 90, 93(b), 97, 103(girl); **Plainpicture**/D Wein p22(t); **Robert Harding Picture Library** p102(b); **Superstock** p52(flag).

These materials may contain links for third party websites. We have no control over, and are not responsible for, the contents of such third party websites. Please use care when accessing them.

Printed and bound in Poland by CGS

2025  2024  2023  2022  2021
22  21  20  19  18  17  16  15